Table of Contents

I am pleased to present this four-year retrospective report on the Troubled Asset Relief Program (TARP). This report provides a status update through December 31, 2012 on our efforts to wind down TARP and recover the taxpayers' outstanding investments.

TARP was created more than four years ago by the Emergency Economic Stabilization Act of 2008 (EESA) as part of a broad-based federal response to the financial crisis. Thanks to TARP and the other emergency actions taken by the government, as well as the financial reforms that are being put in place, our economy is stronger, banks are better capitalized, the weakest parts of the financial system no longer exist, struggling homeowners have seen relief, and credit is more available to consumers and small businesses.

TARP was always meant to be a temporary, emergency program. The government should not be in the business of owning stakes in private companies for an indefinite period of time. That's why, after we extinguished the immediate financial fire, we began moving to exit our investments and replace temporary government support with private capital. During the past year, Treasury's Office of Financial Stability (OFS) made significant strides toward winding down TARP and recovering the taxpayers' outstanding investments. When 2012 began, Treasury held $121 billion in outstanding TARP investments. By the end of 2012, Treasury held just over $40 billion, representing a reduction of more than 66 percent in 12 months. Several highlights from 2012 include:

- On December 14, 2012, Treasury sold its final shares of AIG common stock. With the proceeds from that offering, taxpayers have now realized an overall positive return of $22.7 billion from the Federal Reserve and Treasury's combined commitment to stabilize AIG during the financial crisis.

- OFS substantially reduced the number of banks that remain part of TARP's Capital Purchase Program. At the beginning of 2012, Treasury had outstanding investments of approximately $17 billion in 371 banks. By year's end, we had outstanding investments of approximately $8 billion in 212 banks. Taxpayers have already earned more than $23 billion in positive returns from their investments through TARP's bank programs. At this point, every dollar recovered from those programs represents an additional dollar of positive returns for taxpayers.

- On December 21, 2012, General Motors (GM) repurchased 200 million shares of the company's common stock from Treasury for proceeds of approximately $5.5 billion. The sale took place in connection with Treasury's announcement on December 19, 2012 that we intended to sell our remaining shares in GM within the next 12-15 months, subject to market conditions.

- OFS also substantially wound down TARP's credit market programs during 2012. On January 24, 2012, we completed the wind down of the Small Business Administration 7(a) Securities Purchase Program, collecting $9 million more than we disbursed. Treasury fully recovered its loan under the Term Asset-Backed Securities Loan Facility just after the end of 2012. We are also continuing to wind down the Legacy Securities Public-Private Investment Program. As of December 31, 2012, we had collected approximately 93 percent of the capital invested. Five of the program's funds have now wound down, leaving four in the program.

While TARP's investment programs are winding down, OFS continues its commitment to homeowners by implementing TARP's housing programs to prevent avoidable foreclosures. So far, these programs have directly helped more than 1.5 million homeowners avoid foreclosure, while setting new standards for the mortgage servicing industry, thereby helping millions more.

We have more work to do to further strengthen our economy. However, because the government acted with overwhelming force and speed to put out the financial fires during the crisis, we are in a far better position to confront our economic challenges in the months and years ahead.

Sincerely,

Timothy G. Massad
Assistant Secretary
Office of Financial Stability

When TARP was created, some questioned whether it would succeed in stabilizing the financial system. Many others thought that taxpayers would incur hundreds of billions of dollars in losses on the program. However, by any reasonable standard, TARP worked: it helped stop widespread financial panic, it helped prevent what could have been a devastating collapse of our financial system, and it helped many struggling homeowners keep their homes. Moreover, TARP's cost will be much lower than most people expected when it was created.

During 2012, OFS continued to focus on winding down TARP. By the end of 2012, Treasury had collected nearly 93 percent of the total funds disbursed ($418 billion) under TARP, and many of the taxpayers' investments under the program had yielded positive returns. As a result, the net cost of TARP is now projected to be $55.5 billion – significantly lower than the $700 billion originally authorized by Congress under EESA or the more than $350 billion originally estimated by the Congressional Budget Office. And when Treasury's other interests in AIG[1] are factored in, Treasury estimates that the combined net cost will be approximately $38 billion.

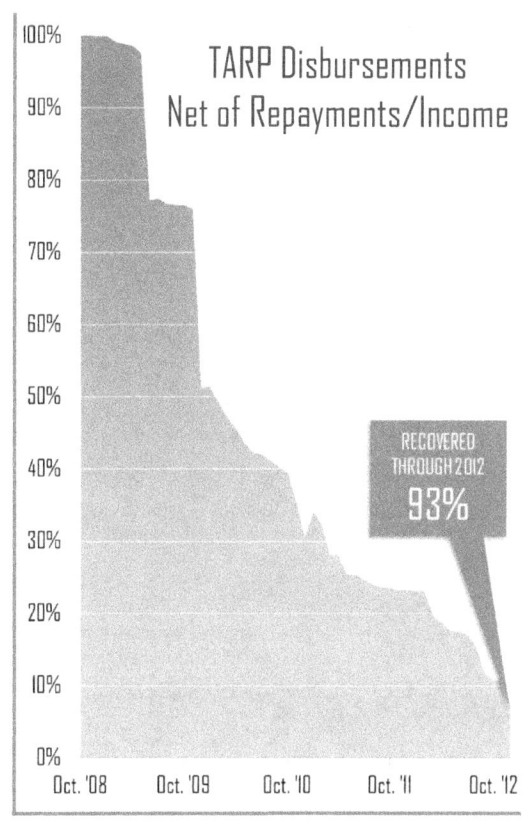

The investment programs under TARP collectively, together with Treasury's overall AIG holdings, are expected to break even or yield a small gain when they are fully wound down. Therefore, the total program cost of TARP is expected to be roughly equal to the amount that is ultimately disbursed to help homeowners avoid foreclosure—money that was never intended to be returned. Moreover, the latest estimates available indicate that the overall financial stability programs that Treasury, the Federal Reserve, and the Federal Deposit Insurance Corporation (FDIC) put in place during the crisis are likely to result in an overall positive financial return for taxpayers in terms of direct fiscal cost.

While Treasury is moving to wind down TARP's investment programs, OFS is also continuing to implement TARP's housing programs. To date, there have been more than 1.5 million homeowner assistance actions taken through the Making Home Affordable (MHA) program. In 2012, more than 350,000 homeowner assistance actions were taken under Treasury's housing programs to help families avoid foreclosure. MHA has also set new standards across the mortgage servicing industry, thereby helping millions more.

---

[1] Treasury's investment in AIG common shares consisted of shares acquired in exchange for preferred stock purchased with TARP funds (TARP shares) and shares received from the trust created by the FRBNY for the benefit of Treasury as a result of its loan to AIG (non-TARP shares).

This is the third retrospective report on TARP that OFS has published. In October 2010, OFS published the TARP Two Year Retrospective,[2] which contains a comprehensive history of each TARP program. The following year, OFS published a Three Year Anniversary Report,[3] which serves as a supplement to the Two Year Retrospective. This report is intended to serve as an update on OFS's efforts to wind down TARP's investment programs and a status update on TARP's housing programs.

TARP'S BANKING INVESTMENT PROGRAMS

Capital Purchase Program (CPP)	Treasury is winding down the CPP through a combination of (1) repayments; (2) restructurings; and (3) sales. Overall, the remaining principal amount invested has been reduced to approximately $7 billion from $205 billion and the program has already generated a positive return to date of more than $15 billion, with additional collections expected moving forward.
Asset Guarantee Program (AGP)	All guarantees were terminated in 2009. No losses were incurred. To date, the positive return on the AGP for taxpayers is more than $4 billion.
Targeted Investment Program (TIP)	All funds disbursed under the TIP were repaid in full in 2009 – plus an additional lifetime positive return of more than $3 billion.
Community Development Capital Initiative (CDCI)	Treasury has a remaining investment of approximately $533 million through the CDCI – less than one percent of its overall bank investments. Treasury will make decisions regarding the CDCI at a later date.
Capital Assistance Program (CAP)	No funding was ever disbursed under the CAP, which was part of the successful stress test process that federal banking regulators conducted in 2009.

CREDIT MARKET PROGRAMS

Term Asset-Backed Securities Loan Facility (TALF)	TARP's remaining credit support agreement was terminated in January 2013 and TALF has earned a positive return for taxpayers. To date, Treasury has realized a positive return of $173 million – with additional income expected moving forward.
Legacy Securities Public-Private Investment Program (PPIP)	As of December 2012, no new investments were permitted. As of January 2013, Treasury had fully recovered its original investment of $18.6 billion in the PPIP, plus a positive return of $331 million through equity and debt repayments, interest, and proceeds in excess of original equity capital, including warrant proceeds. Five of the nine PPIP funds have already been wound down with a net positive return for taxpayers. The total outstanding investments for the remaining four PPIP funds also continue to decline. Consistent with the terms of the program, individual fund managers will make independent determinations about how quickly those remaining four funds are wound down.
SBA 7(a) Securities Purchase Program	The wind down was completed in January 2012. All securities have been sold. Treasury fully recovered the funds invested plus an additional gain of $9 million.

---

[2] http://www.treasury.gov/initiatives/financial-stability/reports/Documents/TARP%20Two%20Year%20Retrospective_10%2005%2010_transmittal%20letter.pdf

[3] http://www.treasury.gov/initiatives/financial-stability/news-room/news/Documents/TARP%20Three%20Year%20Anniversary%20Report.pdf

AUTOMOTIVE INDUSTRY FINANCING PROGRAM

Chrysler

Treasury fully exited its investment in Chrysler Group LLC in July 2011. Treasury has recovered more than 90 percent ($11.1 billion) of the funds committed to stabilize Chrysler ($12.4 billion). Treasury is unlikely to fully recover the difference of $1.3 billion. Treasury has the right to recover proceeds from the disposition of the liquidation trust associated with the bankruptcy of Old Chrysler, but does not expect a material recovery from those assets.

GM

By the end of 2012, Treasury had sold more than two-thirds (612 million shares) of the shares of General Motors common stock it originally held (912 million shares). In December 2012, Treasury announced its intention to fully exit its remaining investment (300 million shares) in GM within 12-15 months, subject to market conditions. In January 2013, it entered into a prearranged written trading plan to proceed with that December 2012 announcement. The total funds Treasury recovers from its GM investment will depend upon future market conditions.

Ally Financial

In May 2012, Treasury outlined its exit strategy for its investment in Ally Financial. Treasury has already recovered about one-third of the total $17 billion invested, and it expects to begin to monetize its remaining investment as the company completes two critical strategic initiatives: the Chapter 11 proceeding for its mortgage subsidiary, Residential Capital, LLC, and the sale of its international auto finance operations. In November 2012, Ally announced that it had reached an agreement to sell its remaining international operations and that it expected total proceeds from those transactions of $9.2 billion.

INVESTMENT IN AIG

AIG

Treasury sold its final shares of AIG common stock in December 2012. Treasury and the Federal Reserve fully recovered the combined $182 billion committed to stabilize the company during the financial crisis plus an additional positive return of $22.7 billion.

TARP'S HOUSING PROGRAMS

MHA

Through December 31, 2012, there were nearly 1.5 million homeowner assistance actions granted through MHA to help struggling homeowners avoid foreclosure. By changing the industry's practices and setting standards for modifications, the program has helped millions more.

HHF

Programs are fully operational in all 18 states and the District of Columbia and saw substantial growth during 2012, both in terms of homeowners served and dollars spent. As a result of recent program and operational changes made by state housing finance agencies working closely with Treasury, OFS expects the pace of assistance to continue to accelerate throughout 2013.

Winding Down TARP's Investment Programs

Treasury's authority to make new commitments under TARP expired on October 3, 2010. Since then, Treasury has been winding down TARP's investment programs and recovering taxpayer dollars. As of December 31, 2012, Treasury had collected through repayments and other income more than $387 billion – or nearly 93 percent – of the $418 billion in TARP funds disbursed to date. The following is an update on OFS's efforts to wind down each TARP investment program as of December 31, 2012.

Banking Investment Programs

During 2012, Treasury continued to wind down TARP's programs to stabilize banks and recover more of the taxpayers' outstanding investments.

Treasury invested approximately $245 billion under TARP to stabilize the nation's banking system through five programs. In the immediate aftermath of the financial crisis, these programs helped to restore confidence in the nation's banking system by bolstering the capital position of banks of all sizes. TARP's banking programs helped to provide these institutions with the additional capital they needed to absorb losses and restart the flow of credit to businesses and consumers. A more comprehensive history of TARP's banking programs can be found in the TARP Two Year Retrospective.[4]

Outstanding Bank Program Investments and Total Returns[5]

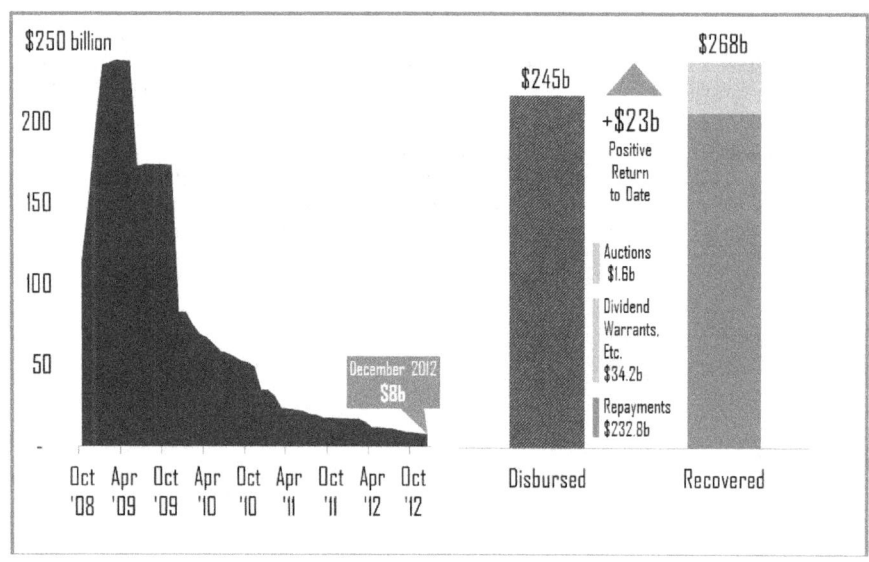

---

[4] http://www.treasury.gov/initiatives/financial-stability/briefing-room/reports/agency_reports/Documents/TARP%20Two%20Year%20Retrospective_10%2005%2010_transmittal%20letter.pdf

[5] Auctions include proceeds from dividends, interest, warrants, and other income where cash has settled with OFS as of December 31, 2012. Repayments are actual collections to date. Includes $2.21 billion in Small Business Lending Fund transfers and $0.36 billion in Community Development Capital Initiative transfers. Note: Write-offs and realized losses total $3.15 billion with a $1.8 billion par value.

These programs have provided a gain for taxpayers. Of the $245 billion originally invested, Treasury has already recovered more than $268 billion through repayments, dividends, interest, warrant sales, and other income as of December 31, 2012 – a positive return of $23 billion. At this point, every additional dollar collected will add to these gains.

Two of TARP's banking programs—the Capital Purchase Program (CPP) and the Community Development Capital Initiative (CDCI)—still have outstanding investments. The other three programs—the Asset Guarantee Program (AGP), the Targeted Investment Program (TIP), and the Capital Assistance Program (CAP)—are now closed.

Capital Purchase Program

The CPP is the largest bank investment program under TARP. Along with TARP's other banking investment programs, the CPP played a key role in stabilizing the financial system.

Treasury initially committed more than a third of the total TARP funding, $250 billion, to the CPP. That amount was ultimately reduced to approximately $205 billion, which was originally invested in more than 450 small and community banks and 22 certified Community Development Financial Institutions (CDFIs). The largest investment was $25 billion and the smallest was $301,000. The final investment under the CPP was made in December 2009. A total of 707 institutions in 48 states, Puerto Rico, and the District of Columbia received investments under the CPP.

Where Things Stand

On January 1, 2012, Treasury had outstanding investments of approximately $17 billion in 371 banks. As of December 31, 2012, Treasury had outstanding investments of approximately $7 billion in 212 banks. At the close of 2012, taxpayers had received $220.44 billion in total income from CPP institutions through repayments, sales, auctions, warrant sales, dividends, interest, and fee income.

On May 3, 2012, Treasury outlined its strategy for winding down the CPP.[6] On December 18, 2012, Treasury provided a status update on the progress achieved toward implementing that strategy.[7] Although many banks have already exited the program, the vast majority of those remaining are small, community institutions. These smaller banks generally are not household names outside the communities they serve. As a result, they sometimes have difficulty raising funds from private investors in the capital markets to repay taxpayers. In addition, like all financial institutions, smaller banks have faced significant challenges in the aftermath of the financial crisis. Many community banks were particularly hard hit by troubled commercial and residential real estate loans.

---

[6] The complete statement by Treasury can be found at: http://www.treasury.gov/connect/blog/Pages/Winding-Down-TARPs-Bank-Programs.aspx

[7] http://www.treasury.gov/connect/blog/Pages/An-Update-on-the-Wind-Down-of-TARP%E2%80%99s-Bank-Programs.aspx

Given those realities, Treasury introduced a three-pronged strategy for winding down the CPP: waiting for some banks to repay at par, restructuring Treasury's investments in limited cases, or selling banking investments to private investors through auctions in cases where the bank is not expected to be able to repay in the near future. Selling these investments can be beneficial for community banks that don't have easy access to the capital markets because the auctions attract new, private capital to replace temporary government support. That enables the government to exit its stake and recover taxpayer dollars, while allowing the bank to keep the capital on its books. The bank can then continue to use that capital to make loans to families and businesses in its local community.

During 2012, 159 CPP institutions exited the program – delivering a total of $8.87 billion in proceeds.[8] Of those 159 institutions, 54 made full repayments at par, 90 were sold through auctions, five were restructured, two exited the program through sales of their assets, and eight entered into bankruptcy or receivership.

As with all TARP investments, Treasury's wind-down plans are subject to market conditions and OFS regularly evaluates its investments in all of the remaining banks.

Repayments at Par

During 2012, 54 financial institutions repaid their CPP investments for proceeds of $6.97 billion including several of the largest remaining investments in the program and the smallest CPP investment of $301,000. As of December 31, 2012, Treasury had received $193.97 billion in repayments under the CPP.[9]

Treasury expects that the majority of the remaining banks that are not auctioned will repay Treasury's CPP preferred shares or subordinated debt at par. Therefore Treasury will continue to hold onto those investments.

Auction Sales

As part of its strategy to wind down the CPP, Treasury has conducted auctions to sell preferred stock and subordinated debt in CPP participants. Treasury generally employs a modified Dutch auction process, which is the same process Treasury uses for warrant auctions, where it establishes a market price by allowing investors to submit bids at specified increments.

Treasury held its first auction of CPP investments in March 2012. By the end of December 2012, Treasury had conducted 12 sets of auctions of preferred stock and subordinated debt in 91 CPP participants, resulting in combined proceeds of more than $1.5 billion for taxpayers.[10] Those 91 banks have also paid more than $300 million in dividends and interest over the life of the investments.

Treasury plans to auction its preferred shares or subordinated debt in approximately two-thirds of the remaining CPP banks in 2013, subject to market conditions.

---

[8] The total of $8.87 billion includes proceeds from some institutions that did not leave the program but partially redeemed their securities.

[9] The total of $193.97 billion in repayments excludes CDCI exchanges from the CPP. The total amount of CPP repayments including CDCI exchanges was $194.32 billion as of December 31, 2012.

[10] Of the 91 institutions that Treasury auctioned its preferred stock and subordinated debt in during 2012, 90 fully exited the CPP.

Restructurings

The final component of Treasury's exit strategy for the CPP is to work with a limited number of banks that are seeking to restructure their Treasury investments. Under these arrangements, Treasury agrees to receive cash or other securities (sometimes at a discount to the original "par" value of the investment), which can be more easily sold.

During 2012, OFS restructured five CPP investments. Treasury agreed to these transactions because they represented the best deal possible for taxpayers. Going forward, Treasury will continue to participate in these types of transactions on a limited basis when it determines that it is in the best interest of taxpayers.

Additional Returns for the Taxpayers

In addition to the preferred shares or debt securities received in exchange for Treasury's investments, Treasury received warrants to purchase common shares or – in the case of private financial institutions – additional preferred or subordinated debt, from the participants at the time of the CPP investment. Treasury also earns dividends or interest on the securities received. These provide taxpayers with additional returns on their investment. During 2012, Treasury received $619 million in additional returns from banks participating in the CPP from warrants, dividends, and interest.

Warrant Repurchases

When a CPP participant repurchases its original investment, it may also repurchase its warrants for common stock at an agreed upon fair market price. If an institution decides not to repurchase its warrants, Treasury has the contractual right to sell them. Treasury has followed a policy of disposing of warrants as soon as practicable if no agreement is reached.

During 2012, Treasury received $144.27 million in total proceeds from the disposition of warrants associated with 100 CPP investments. Of these, 67 were repurchased by the financial institution that issued them and 33 were sold by Treasury through public offerings. Since the start of the CPP, Treasury has realized $7.73 billion in gross proceeds from the sale of these warrants.

The latest information about the sale of warrants under TARP can be found in Treasury's Warrant Disposition Report.[11]

Dividends and Interest

Treasury also collects dividend and interest payments from CPP participants, which add to the total return that taxpayers receive under the program. As of December 31, 2012, the total amount of dividend and interest income that Treasury received from CPP investments (life to date) was $11.84 billion.

Under the terms of the CPP, Treasury has the contractual right to appoint up to two members to the board of directors of a CPP recipient in the event that it misses a sixth dividend or interest payment on the preferred stock or subordinated debt.

---

[11] http://www.treasury.gov/initiatives/financial-stability/reports/Pages/Warrant-Disposition-Reports.aspx

As of December 31, 2012, Treasury had elected a total of 22 directors to the boards of 13 banks. Fifty-two institutions had agreed to have Treasury observers at their board of directors meetings, including several that are expected to miss their sixth dividend payment in the near future.

Treasury issues a monthly report[12] detailing dividends and interest received, as well as missed payments.

Community Development Capital Initiative

To help mitigate the adverse impact that the financial crisis had on communities underserved by traditional banks, Treasury launched the Community Development Capital Initiative (CDCI) in February 2010. Under this program, Treasury provided capital to banks, thrifts, and credit unions that qualified as Community Development Financial Institutions (CDFIs). These investments carried an initial dividend or interest rate of two percent, compared to the five percent rate offered under the CPP.

Recognizing the unique circumstances facing CDFIs to raise capital, the dividend rate was designed to increase to nine percent after eight years, compared to five years for institutions participating in the CPP. CDFIs participating in the CPP that were in good standing were allowed to exchange securities issued under the CPP for securities under the more favorable terms of this program.

Where Things Stand

Treasury completed funding under this program in September 2010. The total investment amount for the program was approximately $570 million for 84 institutions.[13]

During 2012, Treasury received $37.5 million in repayments from six CDCI institutions. As of December 31, 2012, there were 78 institutions remaining in the CDCI program with a total outstanding investment amount of $532.5 million. During 2012, Treasury received $11.16 million in dividends from CDCI institutions. Treasury will announce its plans regarding the program at a later date.

Targeted Investment Program

Treasury established the Targeted Investment Program (TIP) in December 2008 to prevent a loss of confidence in certain financial institutions during the crisis, which could have resulted in significant financial market disruptions. This could have threatened the financial strength of similarly situated financial institutions and undermined the overall economy.

Under the program, Treasury invested $20 billion in Bank of America Corp. (Bank of America) and another $20 billion in Citigroup Inc. (Citigroup). These investments were made in addition to those that these banks received under the CPP. Similar to the CPP, Treasury invested in preferred stock, and received warrants to purchase common stock in each institution under the terms of the TIP.

---

[12] http://www.treasury.gov/initiatives/financial-stability/reports/Pages/Dividends-and-Interest-Reports.aspx

[13] Of this amount, approximately $363.3 million ($355.7 million from principal and $7.6 million from warrants) represented exchanges by 28 banks of investments under the CPP into the CDCI.

In December 2009, both Bank of America and Citigroup repaid their TIP investments in full. Treasury received $3 billion in dividends under the program. Treasury also received warrants from each bank, which provided taxpayers with $1.43 billion in additional gains on their TIP investments. The program is now closed and resulted in a positive return of $4 billion for taxpayers.

Asset Guarantee Program

The Asset Guarantee Program (AGP) was established in late 2008. Conducted jointly by Treasury, the Federal Reserve, and the FDIC, the AGP was used in conjunction with other forms of emergency assistance provided under TARP. Like the TIP, the AGP was designed for financial institutions whose failure could harm the financial system and reduce the potential for spillover to the broader financial system and economy.

Two institutions were given assistance under the AGP – Bank of America[14] and Citigroup. They were selected because of the large number of illiquid assets that both of them held at the time of the financial crisis. Their failures would likely have had a severe impact on the broader financial system. The AGP helped these institutions maintain the confidence of depositors and other funding sources to continue meeting the credit needs of households and businesses.

On December 28, 2012, Treasury received Citigroup trust preferred securities and approximately $183 million in associated dividend and interest payments. Treasury sold those securities in February 2013 for $894 million[15], in addition to receiving another $16 million in dividend and interest payments in January 2013. These transactions added to the positive return that taxpayers have received from their investment in Citigroup under TARP. Since Citigroup made no claims for loss payments to the government and Treasury made no guarantee payments of TARP funds to Citigroup, all payments and income received from the sale of securities have constituted a net gain to taxpayers. The AGP is now closed and has so far resulted in a positive return of more than $4 billion.

Capital Assistance Program

In 2009, Treasury worked with federal banking regulators to develop a comprehensive "stress test" known as the Supervisory Capital Assessment Program (SCAP). The purpose of the SCAP was to determine the health of the nation's 19 largest bank holding companies. This forward-looking stress test provided unprecedented levels of transparency and helped to restore confidence in the banking system.

---

[14] In May 2009, before the transaction was finalized, Bank of America decided to terminate negotiations, and in September 2009, the government and Bank of America entered into an agreement under which Bank of America agreed to pay a termination fee of $425 million to the government, $276 million of which went to Treasury. The fee compensated the government for the value that Bank of America had received from the announcement of the government's willingness to guarantee and share losses on the pool of assets from and after the date of the term sheet. No TARP funds were spent. As a result, this fee was a net gain to taxpayers.

[15] Since this sale occurred after December 31, 2012, it is not reflected in the graphs and charts throughout this report.

In conjunction with the SCAP, Treasury announced that it would provide capital under TARP through the Capital Assistance Program (CAP) to those institutions that needed additional capital but were unable to raise it through private sources. The CAP was offered to all banks and qualifying financial institutions, not solely to those banks that had been subject to the SCAP.

Only one TARP institution, Ally Financial (formerly GMAC), required additional funds under TARP to meet its SCAP requirements but received them through the Automotive Industry Financing Program, not the CAP. The CAP closed on November 9, 2009 without making any investments and did not incur any losses to taxpayers. Following the release of the stress test results, banks were able to raise hundreds of billions of dollars in private capital.

Credit Market Programs

TARP's credit market programs played a key role in helping to restart the markets that provide financing for auto loans, credit cards, mortgages, and small business lending.

In 2008, the government took forceful action to restart credit markets that had come under severe stress during the financial crisis. In particular, three programs were launched under TARP:

- The Legacy Securities Public-Private Investment Program (PPIP), which helped bring private capital back into the market for non-agency residential and commercial mortgage-backed securities;

- The Small Business Administration 7(a) Securities Purchase Program (SBA 7(a) Program), which provided added liquidity to the market for small business lending; and

- The Term Asset-Backed Securities Loan Facility (TALF), a joint program with the Federal Reserve Bank of New York (FRBNY) that helped to restart the markets that provide credit to consumers and small businesses.

Although the specific implementation methods were different for each program, the overall goal of each one was the same—to restart the flow of credit to meet the critical financing needs of small businesses and consumers. These credit market programs under TARP, combined with additional measures taken by the Obama Administration, helped ensure that various types of consumer and small business loans remained available in the immediate aftermath of the financial crisis and in the years since.

In 2012, OFS made considerable progress winding down TARP's credit market programs. The SBA 7(a) Program closed with a small positive return. Treasury's credit protection for TALF was reduced during 2012 and subsequently eliminated in January of 2013. Five of the investment funds under PPIP were wound down, leaving four remaining. Of the approximately $19 billion that was invested through these programs, Treasury has now reduced the amount outstanding for taxpayers to $3.6 billion. The status of each is described below.

Legacy Securities Public-Private Investment Program (PPIP)

Treasury launched PPIP to support credit market functioning and facilitate price discovery in the markets for commercial and residential mortgage financing. Using TARP funds alongside equity capital raised from private investors, PPIP was designed to generate a significant purchasing power and demand for troubled non-agency residential mortgage-backed securities (RMBS) and commercial mortgage-backed securities (CMBS).

PPIP originally consisted of nine public-private investment funds (PPIFs). These funds were established by private sector fund managers to purchase eligible legacy RMBS and CMBS from banks, insurance companies, mutual funds, pension funds, and other eligible sellers as defined under EESA. In implementing the program, fund managers established meaningful partnership roles for small, minority, veteran-, and women-owned businesses. These roles include, among others, asset management, capital-raising, broker-dealer, investment sourcing, research, advisory, cash management, and fund administration services. Collectively, the PPIP fund managers established 10 unique relationships with leading small, minority, veteran-, and women-owned financial services businesses.

Since it was launched in 2009, PPIP has helped to restart the market for these securities by drawing in new, private capital. This in turn has helped more credit become available to consumers and small businesses.

Where Things Stand

At the close of 2012, the PPIFs had drawn down $24.9 billion of the total original capital committed (83 percent of total original purchasing power), which has been invested in eligible assets and cash equivalents. The investment period had ended for all PPIFs and Treasury had received approximately 93 percent of its original $18.6 billion investment, including interest income, gains, and repayments of debt and equity capital.

Treasury's original $18.6 billion investment was fully recovered in January 2013 and taxpayers have received a positive return of $331 million through equity and debt repayments, interest, and proceeds in excess of original equity capital, including warrant proceeds.[16] Treasury expects PPIP to result in more than $2 billion of positive returns for taxpayers.

The following is a summary of the status of individual PPIFs as of December 31, 2012[17]:

PPIFs (in billions as of December 31, 2012)	Total Obligations	Amount Outstanding	Total Cash Back
Alliance Bernstein	$ 3.28	$ 0.00	$ 3.74
Angelo, Gordon & Co., LP and GE Capital Real Estate	$ 3.48	$ 0.72	$ 2.89
BlackRock, Inc	$ 1.75	$ 0.00	$ 2.01
Invesco Ltd.	$ 1.74	$ 0.00	$ 1.90
Marathon Asset Management, LP	$ 1.42	$ 0.74	$ 0.76
Oaktree Capital Management, LP	$ 3.48	$ 0.77	$ 0.95
RLJ Western Asset Management, LP	$ 1.86	$ 0.00	$ 2.33
The TCW Group, Inc	$ 0.36	$ 0.00	$ 0.38
Wellington Management Company, LLP	$ 3.45	$ 1.37	$ 2.29
Total	$ 20.82	$ 3.59	$ 17.24

Although the program was designed so that funds could remain invested until 2019, the program's success has led the asset managers to wind down the funds earlier than originally expected. Five of these funds – UST/TCW Senior Mortgage Securities Fund, L.P.; Invesco Legacy Securities Master Fund, L.P.; AllianceBernstein Legacy Securities Master Fund, L.P.; RLJ Western Asset Public/Private Master Fund, L.P.; and Blackrock PPIF, L.P. – have already been wound down and exited the program, providing a gain to taxpayers. Four others – AG GECC PPIF Master Fund, L.P.; Marathon Legacy Securities Public-Private Investment Partnership, L.P.; Oaktree PPIP Fund,

---

[16] Any returns received in January 2013 are not included in the charts in this report.

[17] Includes both public and private funds.

L.P.; and Wellington Management Legacy Securities PPIF Master Fund, LP – have made substantial progress in doing so.

Treasury produces a PPIP quarterly report[18] that provides detailed information on the funds and their investments and returns. It is typically released several weeks after the end of each quarter.

SBA 7(a) Securities Purchase Program

Treasury launched the SBA 7(a) Program as part of the Obama Administration's efforts to help small businesses in the wake of the financial crisis. This program was aimed at helping the secondary market for small business loans recover and free up credit for small businesses.

Under this program, Treasury purchased securities comprised of the guaranteed portion of SBA 7(a) loans, which finance a wide range of small business needs, including working capital, machinery, equipment, furniture, and fixtures. This enabled small businesses across the country to continue their day-to-day operations and making investments needed to grow.

From March through September of 2010, Treasury made open market purchases from participating pool assemblers of SBA 7(a) securities. Through its purchases, Treasury injected much needed liquidity into this market to help restart the flow of credit, enabling pool assemblers to purchase additional small business loans from loan originators. Since Treasury began its purchases, the SBA 7(a) market has recovered with new SBA 7(a) loan volumes returning to pre-crisis levels.

Where Things Stand

On January 24, 2012, Treasury completed the fifth and final disposition of securities within the SBA 7(a) Securities Purchase Program,[19] marking the successful wind down of the program. Treasury collected a total of $376 million through the program. These cash collections exceeded Treasury's original investment amount by $9 million.[20]

The SBA 7(a) Program is now closed.

Term Asset-Backed Securities Loan Facility

The third credit market program under TARP is the Term Asset-Backed Securities Loan Facility (TALF). TALF supported the issuance of nearly 3 million auto loans, more than 1 million student loans, nearly 900,000 small business loans, 150,000 other types of business loans, and millions of credit card loans.

Under TALF, the FRBNY lent funds to investors of these types of securities. By encouraging the issuance of ABS and CMBS, TALF helped support the economy by increasing credit availability to American households and businesses.

---

[18] http://www.treasury.gov/initiatives/financial-stability/reports/Pages/Public-Private-Investment-Program-Quarterly-Report.aspx

[19] Additional information can be found at : http://www.treasury.gov/press-center/press-releases/Pages/tg1398.aspx

[20] Treasury originally invested a total of $367 million, excluding purchased accrued interest.

As part of the program, Treasury originally pledged $20 billion in credit protection through TARP against potential losses on TALF loans. In light of repayments over time and the reduction in the number of TALF loans outstanding, Treasury's credit protection commitment was subsequently reduced to $4.3 billion in June 2010 and to $1.4 billion in June 2012.

Where Things Stand

As of December 31, 2012, the accumulated fees collected through TALF ($856 million)[21] exceeded the total principal amount of TALF loans outstanding ($556 million). Therefore, in January 2013, Treasury and the Federal Reserve determined that Treasury's commitment of TARP funds to provide credit protection was no longer considered necessary. In addition, the early repayment of TALF loans has allowed the $100 million in temporary loans that Treasury made over the course of the program under its credit protection commitment to be repaid in full with $13 million in interest.

TALF remains a joint Treasury-Federal Reserve program. Given that Treasury's investment has been repaid in full with interest, each additional dollar Treasury collects through TALF going forward represents an additional gain for taxpayers. The final TALF loan is scheduled to mature on March 30, 2015. All loans remain well collateralized and current in payments of principal and interest. Treasury and the FRBNY do not expect any cost to taxpayers from TALF.

---

[21] This amount includes the original $100 million in temporary loans that Treasury made during the program as part of its credit protection commitment.

Automotive Industry Financing Program

TARP prevented a collapse of the American automotive industry, saving an estimated one million jobs. Today GM and Chrysler are more competitive and viable companies. Moreover, since June 2009, the auto industry has added more than a quarter of a million new jobs.

The Automotive Industry Financing Program (AIFP) was launched under TARP to prevent a collapse of the American automotive industry. The severe condition of the industry at that time posed a significant risk to financial market stability and threatened the overall economy.

It began in December 2008 when President Bush extended short-term emergency loans to GM and Chrysler. These two automakers were the most severely impacted by the crisis. When President Obama took office, he decided to provide additional investment only if the companies engaged in fundamental restructuring. Both companies were required to develop plans to achieve long-term viability, under which all stakeholders, including unions, dealers, creditors, and others, would make substantial sacrifices.

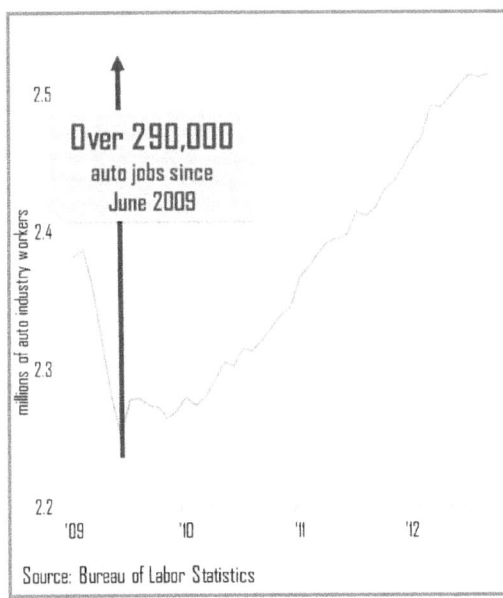

Over 290,000 auto jobs since June 2009

Source: Bureau of Labor Statistics

Treasury provided nearly $80 billion in loans and equity investments under the AIFP. Assistance was provided to GM, Chrysler, and their financing entities. Treasury also provided loans to ensure that auto suppliers would be compensated for their parts and services that had already been purchased by the auto companies.

While the industry continues to face challenges, GM, Chrysler, and Ford have returned to profitability. An estimated one million jobs were saved by the assistance provided under TARP. This assistance made it possible for them to restructure and compete more effectively. As a result, since 2009 the auto industry has continued to rebound.

Of the approximately $80 billion that was provided to the auto industry under TARP, Treasury has now recovered $46.40 billion. As of December 31, 2012, Treasury held 300.1 million shares of GM common stock, representing approximately 22 percent (or less than 19 percent on a fully diluted basis) of the outstanding shares of common stock in the company. Treasury also held 74 percent of the common equity and $5.9 billion of mandatorily convertible preferred stock in Ally. Treasury has already exited its investments in Chrysler and Chrysler Financial.

The process of rescuing GM and Chrysler was done through the standard procedures of the nation's bankruptcy courts and both restructurings were found to have been conducted in accordance with well settled law.

While the cost of the auto industry's rescue under TARP will not be known until the remaining investments are liquidated, it is currently projected to cost $20.26 billion. However, the cost of disorderly liquidations of GM and Chrysler, and the effects those would have had on the industry and the nation as a whole would have been far higher.

General Motors

Treasury provided approximately $50 billion of TARP funds to GM in 2008 and 2009. Since then, GM has gone through a managed bankruptcy and is now a more competitive company. Treasury's investment in GM was originally made in the form of loans, some of which were subsequently converted into common and preferred stock. Treasury currently holds only common stock.

Where Things Stand

By the end of 2012, Treasury had sold more than two-thirds (612 million) of the 912 million shares of GM common stock it originally held. In December 2012, Treasury announced its intention to fully exit its remaining GM investment within 12-15 months, subject to market conditions. OFS believes that moving to exit the remaining GM investments within this timeframe is consistent with Treasury's dual goals of winding down TARP as soon as practicable and protecting taxpayer interests.

The first step in that plan took place on December 21, 2012, when GM purchased 200 million shares of the company's common stock from Treasury at $27.50 per share for a total of $5.5 billion.[22] This repurchase reduced Treasury's total number of remaining shares of GM common stock to 300.1 million. The disposition of those common shares began in January 2013 pursuant to a pre-arranged written trading plan. The manner, amount, and timing of the sales under the plan are subject to market conditions.

Chrysler

Treasury committed a total of $12.4 billion to Chrysler under TARP.

The Obama Administration determined that Chrysler could achieve viability by partnering with the international car company Fiat. As part of the planned restructuring, in April 2009, Chrysler filed for bankruptcy protection. In May 2009, Treasury provided $1.9 billion to Chrysler (Old Chrysler) under a debtor-in-possession financing agreement for assistance during its bankruptcy proceeding.

In June 2009 a newly formed entity, Chrysler Group LLC (New Chrysler) acquired most of Old Chrysler's assets through a court-authorized sale. Since then, Chrysler has lowered its structural costs, adopted new technologies, rejuvenated its product line, and rebuilt its brands.

Where Things Stand

In July 2011, Treasury fully exited its investment in Chrysler, six years ahead of schedule. Of the $12.4 billion disbursed to Chrysler under TARP, Treasury recovered more than $11.1 billion for taxpayers through principal repayments, interest, and cancelled commitments. Treasury is unlikely to fully recover the difference of $1.3 billion owed by Old Chrysler.

---

[22] Additional information can be found in Treasury's press release: http://www.treasury.gov/press-center/press-releases/Pages/tg1810.aspx

Ally Financial

Treasury also made a $17.2 billion investment in Ally Financial (formerly GMAC) under TARP. The company has been the primary source of financing for GM's dealers and consumers for more than 90 years. Subsequently, after Treasury's investment, Ally became a primary source of financing for Chrysler dealers. Supporting Ally made it possible for GM and Chrysler dealers to continue providing car loans to their customers and secure financing to run their businesses during the financial crisis.

As of December 31, 2012, Treasury had recovered approximately one-third ($5.8 billion) of its original $17.2 billion investment. Treasury expects to begin monetizing its remaining investment as the company completes two critical strategic initiatives: the Chapter 11 proceeding for its mortgage subsidiary, Residential Capital, LLC (ResCap) and the sale of its international auto finance operations. In November 2012, Ally announced that it had reached an agreement to sell its remaining international operations and that it expected total proceeds from those transactions of $9.2 billion.

Where Things Stand

On May 14, 2012, Assistant Secretary Timothy Massad issued a statement on the ResCap Chapter 11 filing in which he stated that by addressing the legacy mortgage liabilities at ResCap, which are old loans made during the days before the housing bubble burst, taxpayers will be in a stronger position to recover their remaining investment in Ally.[23]

By the end of 2012, ResCap had made significant progress toward bringing its Chapter 11 bankruptcy proceedings to a successful conclusion. Ally's sales of its international operations are also due to close at various times over the course of 2013.

As these two key initiatives are completed, Treasury will be able to recover more of its remaining investment through sales of its stock (either through public or private sales) or through further sales of assets. How those sales options develop will depend on the progress of Ally's two strategic initiatives, market conditions, and other factors.

---

[23] The full statement by Assistant Secretary Massad can be accessed at: http://www.treasury.gov/connect/blog/Pages/Putting-Taxpayers-in-a-Stronger-Position-to-Continue-Recovering-Their-Investment-in-Ally-Financial.aspx

Investment in American International Group (AIG)

Treasury and the Federal Reserve provided assistance to AIG because the consequences of a company of its size and scope failing at that time, in those circumstances, would have had far-reaching and catastrophic consequences for the economy and American families and businesses. By the end of 2012, Treasury had sold its final shares of AIG common stock. Moreover, Treasury and the Federal Reserve fully recovered the original $182 billion commitment made to stabilize the company during the financial crisis – plus an additional positive return of $22.7 billion.

On December 11, 2012, Treasury announced the sale of its final shares of AIG common stock. Including the proceeds from this latest offering, the overall positive return on the Federal Reserve and Treasury's combined $182 billion commitment to stabilize AIG during the financial crisis is now $22.7 billion.

Treasury's AIG Common Stock Position Since January 2011

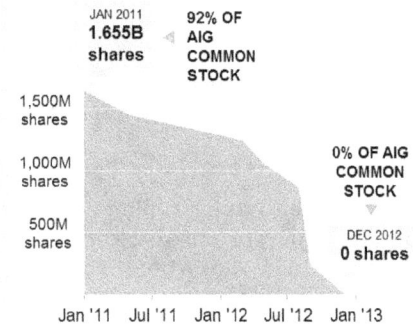

AIG's Total Assets

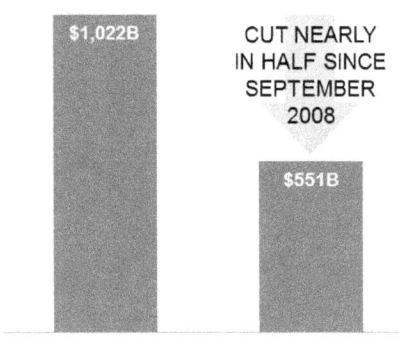

September 2008   September 2012

SOURCE: TREASURY & AIG

+$22.7 BILLION
The overall positive return for taxpayers on the Treasury and Federal Reserve's original $182 billion commitment to AIG.

1.655 BILLION
The number of shares of AIG common stock Treasury has sold over the last two years.

+$9.5 BILLION
The profit on the Maiden Lane II and III special purpose vehicles, which purchased mortgage-related assets from AIG and its counterparties.

46 PERCENT
Reduction in the size of the company by assets since 2008. By streamlining its operations and focusing on its core insurance business, the size of AIG has been cut nearly in half

MORE THAN 90 PERCENT
Reduction in the notional size of the legacy derivatives portfolio at AIG Financial Products, which is being wound down.

During the financial crisis, Treasury and the Federal Reserve committed approximately $182 billion to prevent the collapse of AIG. That amount included $70 billion[24] that Treasury committed through TARP as well as $112 billion committed by the FRBNY.

At the time, AIG was the largest provider of conventional insurance in the world. Millions of Americans depended on it for their life savings and it had a substantial presence in many critical financial markets, including municipal bonds.

The same pressures that caused the failure of Lehman Brothers in September 2008 brought AIG to the brink of collapse. It became clear that AIG had massive liquidity needs and was facing the potential for huge losses. Imprudent risk-taking during better times in the years preceding the financial crisis meant that when the financial cycle turned downward, AIG had hundreds of billions of dollars in commitments without the assets to back them up. As AIG teetered on the brink of bankruptcy, confidence in the financial system as a whole was eroding. Firms were trying to shore up their balance sheets by selling risky assets and hoarding cash.

> *"Congress granted the Federal Reserve emergency authority precisely so that the government had some capacity to act to contain a systemic financial crisis. To not to have used that authority at that time would have been deeply irresponsible."*
>
> Secretary Timothy Geithner on the government's rescue of AIG
> January, 2010

Panic began spreading and pressures spilled over to virtually all credit markets. These events had immediate economic consequences for all Americans, potentially affecting everything from public works projects by state and local governments to school construction, hospital operations, and the transportation of goods throughout the country. Therefore, over the following six months, Treasury and the FRBNY took a series of steps to prevent AIG's disorderly failure and mitigate risks to the financial system and the broader economy.

Where Things Stand

At the time the government provided assistance to AIG, most people thought that those funds would not be recovered. However, since the financial crisis, AIG has dramatically restructured, enabling it to fully repay taxpayers. The size of the company has been cut nearly in half as it sold non-core assets and focused on its core insurance operations. AIG's Financial Products unit is continuing to be wound down and has cut its legacy derivatives exposure by more than 90 percent to date.

As a result of the combined efforts of AIG, Treasury, and the Federal Reserve, the $182 billion committed to stabilize the company has been fully recovered – plus an additional positive return of $22.7 billion. Treasury continues to hold warrants to purchase approximately 2.7 million shares of AIG common stock – the sale of which will provide an additional positive return to taxpayers.

Treasury will continue to wind down its remaining investment related to AIG in a way that balances exiting as soon as practicable with maximizing value for taxpayers.

---

[24] $2 billion of which was never drawn.

Housing Initiatives Under TARP

Treasury, in collaboration with the U.S. Department of Housing and Urban Development (HUD) and the Federal Housing Finance Agency (FHFA), established several programs to help struggling homeowners avoid foreclosure. So far, there have been nearly 1.5 million homeowner assistance actions through these programs. These programs have also set new standards across the mortgage servicing industry that have indirectly helped millions more.

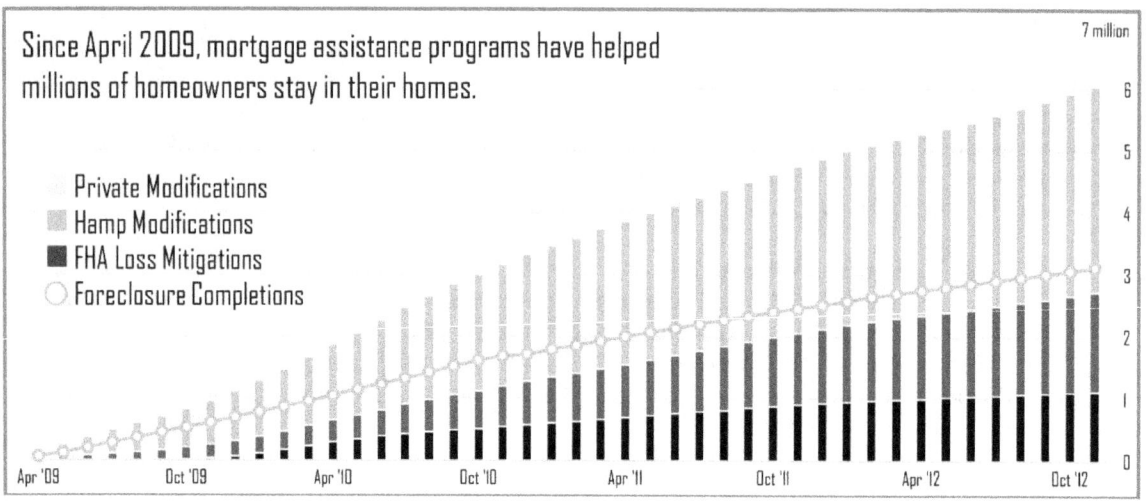

In February 2009, President Obama announced a number of steps to strengthen the housing market and help struggling homeowners avoid foreclosure. As part of this broad response to the housing crisis, Treasury under TARP established two central programs, Making Home Affordable® (MHA) and the Hardest Hit Fund® (HHF).

Making Home Affordable® (MHA)

Launched in February 2009, MHA consists of several programs designed to help struggling homeowners prevent avoidable foreclosures. MHA's principal component is the Home Affordable Modification Program (HAMP®). As the housing crisis evolved, Treasury launched several specialized programs to help homeowners find a solution that is right for their situation.

Through December 31, 2012, there were nearly 1.5 million homeowner assistance actions granted through MHA, consisting of first-and second-lien permanent modifications, Home Affordable Foreclosure Alternatives (HAFA) transactions, and Unemployment Program (UP) forbearance plans. During 2012 there were more than 430,000 actions taken under MHA to help families prevent a possible foreclosure.

Home Affordable Modification Program (HAMP)®

The cornerstone of MHA is the Home Affordable Modification Program (HAMP)®, which permanently modifies first-lien mortgages for eligible borrowers to a more affordable monthly payment to prevent a foreclosure. HAMP helps homeowners who face a serious financial hardship, have a high debt-to-income ratio, and demonstrate the ability to sustain their monthly mortgage payments after a modification has been granted.

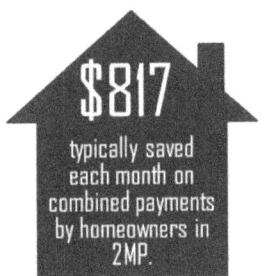

$545 typically saved each month by homeowners in active HAMP permanent modifications.

As of December 31, 2012, more than 1.1 million homeowners have received permanent HAMP modifications. Homeowners in active HAMP permanent modifications typically save more than $500 per month, which is more than one-third of what they were paying before their modification. Since HAMP began, homeowners in permanent modifications have saved an estimated $17.3 billion in monthly mortgage payments.

OFS also implements two smaller programs within HAMP – the Principal Reduction Alternative (PRA) and the Second Lien Modification Program (2MP).

Principal Reduction Alternative (PRA)

Under the PRA, servicers of non-government sponsored enterprises (GSE) loans are required to evaluate the benefit of principal reduction for mortgages with a loan-to-value ratio of 115 percent or greater when evaluating a homeowner for a HAMP first-lien modification. Although servicers are not required to reduce principal as part of the modification, the program provides incentives for them to do so.

As of December 31, 2012, there had been more than 118,000 permanent HAMP modifications with some form of principal reduction. These modifications typically reduced the principal amount by $66,719 or nearly one-third of the principal balance before modification.

Second Lien Modification Program (2MP)

$817 typically saved each month on combined payments by homeowners in 2MP.

Many homeowners have had their first liens modified but continue struggling to keep up with payments for a second lien on the same property. Under the 2MP, Treasury provides incentives for second-lien holders to modify or extinguish these mortgages when the first-lien mortgage for the same property has been permanently modified under HAMP.®

As of December 31, 2012, more than 103,000 homeowners in a permanent first-lien modification under HAMP had received assistance through 2MP. Homeowners in 2MP typically save nearly $817 per month on their combined first and second lien monthly mortgage payments. More than 50 percent of the borrowers benefiting from 2MP reside in three states: California (36 percent), Florida (nine percent), and New York (seven percent).

Setting New Standards

HAMP's impact has gone far beyond the number of homeowners who have received direct assistance under the program. It has set new standards and changed industry practices in fundamental ways, and thereby helped millions more families stay in their homes.

There were very few private modifications taking place before HAMP was launched. Many of those that occurred did not lower payments.[25] This is because there were no standards in the mortgage industry as to how to make modifications affordable and sustainable. HAMP provided such standards. These include using a target debt-to-income ratio as the standard for determining an affordable mortgage payment and a net present value test to determine whether the modification makes economic sense for the holder of the mortgage. Partly as a result of these new standards, the proportion of private loan modifications that reduce monthly payments for homeowners has more than doubled. Together, public and private efforts have helped approximately six million Americans get mortgage assistance to prevent avoidable foreclosures.

HAMP has also set important new consumer protection standards. Before HAMP, the mortgage industry was ill-equipped to handle the overwhelming number of homeowners in need of assistance. To address this shortcoming, Treasury required mortgage servicers that volunteered to participate in HAMP to overhaul their operations and adopt new practices for assisting homeowners seeking help. These include:

- Requiring the largest participating mortgage servicers to establish a single point of contact (SPOC) for homeowners who are potentially eligible for MHA to ensure that a single, knowledgeable case manager can guide them through the entire application and resolution process. On November 14, 2012, Treasury released a special report detailing the steps Treasury and other federal agencies have taken to get the mortgage industry to improve customer service in the MHA program, including through SPOC requirements.[26]

- Requiring participating mortgage servicers to limit the practice of "dual tracking" – where mortgage servicers begin the foreclosure process while simultaneously evaluating homeowners for assistance; and

- Requiring participating mortgage servicers to provide qualified unemployed homeowners with a forbearance period of up to 12 months, subject to investor and regulator guidelines, during which their monthly payments are temporarily reduced or suspended while they look for work.

MHA continues to maintain a comprehensive compliance program to make sure that participating servicers are following the program's guidelines with respect to how they evaluate and assist homeowners. In 2011, Treasury expanded its public reporting to disclose how participating mortgage servicers are complying with program guidelines. Treasury provides information about servicer performance through two types of data:

- Quarterly compliance data, which reflects servicer compliance with specific MHA guidelines; and

- Program results data, which reflects how timely and effectively servicers assist eligible homeowners and report program activity.

---

[25] At the end of 2008, the Office of the Comptroller of the Currency (OCC) reported that the majority of loan modifications made that year did not reduce monthly payments. Nearly 27 percent resulted in unchanged monthly payments, and about 32 percent increased monthly payments. More information can found at: http://www.occ.gov/publications/publications-by-type/other-publications-reports/mortgage-metrics-q4-2008/index-mortgage-metrics-q4-2008.html

[26] The full report can be accessed at: http://www.treasury.gov/initiatives/financial-stability/reports/Documents/SPOC%20Special%20Report_Final.pdf.

The following three charts show how participating servicers have performed on three key metrics. The results show that servicers are focusing attention on areas identified in previous program reviews and, as a result, are demonstrating continued improvement in program implementation.

- The first chart shows the percentage of loans where the servicer assessment did not concur with those of Treasury's compliance agent for MHA (MHA-C).

- The second chart shows the percentage of loans where MHA-C was unable to draw a conclusion on the servicer's MHA determination.

- The third shows the percentage of loans for which MHA-C's income calculation differs from that of the servicer's by more than five percent.

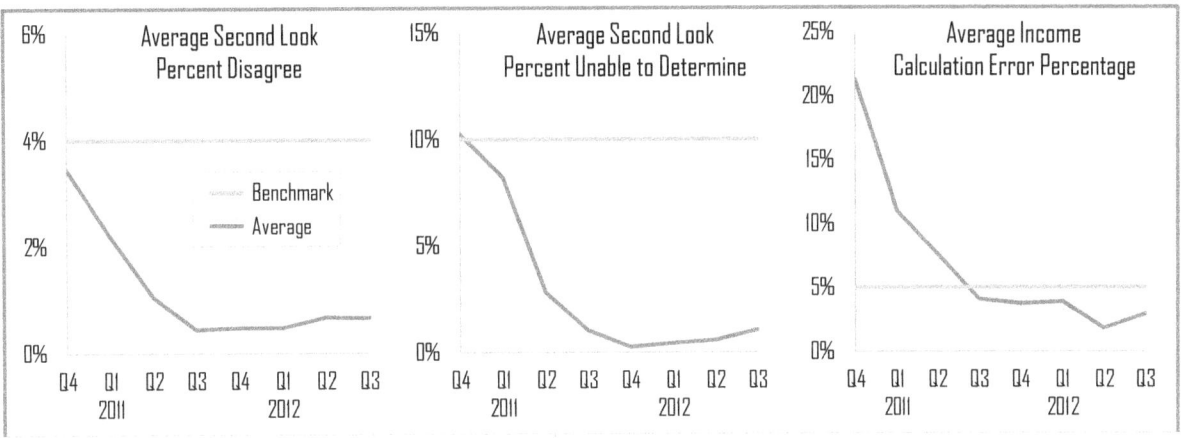

Settlement with Mortgage Servicers

MHA's mortgage servicing standards also served as the basis for the National Mortgage Settlement between 49 state attorneys general, the Federal Government, and the country's five largest mortgage loan servicers (Ally/GMAC, Bank of America, Citigroup, JPMorgan Chase, and Wells Fargo).

The settlement was intended to provide as much as $25 billion in relief to distressed borrowers and direct payments to states and the Federal Government. The agreement settled certain alleged violations of state and federal law based on the mortgage loan servicing activities of the country's five largest mortgage loan servicers, including claims of document-related foreclosure abuses. Treasury provided advice during the settlement negotiations and shared knowledge gained through implementation of the Administration's foreclosure prevention programs, including MHA.

MHA's borrower protections have been widely adopted by the industry and were included as part of the national mortgage settlement. They have also served as the basis for rules being developed by the Consumer Financial Protection Bureau (CFPB) and scheduled to become effective in 2013. MHA has also helped to standardize short sale procedures with the GSEs, creating a legacy of new standards that the CFPB will be responsible for monitoring in the future.

Additional information can be found at the dedicated website established by the attorneys general on the Executive Committee who negotiated the settlement.[27]

---

[27] http://nationalmortgagesettlement.com/

Home Affordable Foreclosure Alternatives Program (HAFA)

For some homeowners, a mortgage modification is not the right solution. To help these homeowners, Treasury developed the Home Affordable Foreclosure Alternatives Program (HAFA) so they can still avoid foreclosure. HAFA's goal is to help homeowners exit their homes and transition to a more affordable living situation through a short sale or deed-in-lieu of foreclosure. HAFA provides a defined process along with incentives to encourage these transactions.

As of December 31, 2012, more than 124,000 homeowners had reached agreements with their servicer to exit their home under the HAFA Program. More than 101,000 had completed a short sale or deed-in-lieu of foreclosure. HAFA provides $3,000 for relocation assistance after a homeowner exits their home.

Home Affordable Unemployment Program (UP)

Treasury has also developed a program to provide temporary relief for homeowners who struggle to keep up with their mortgage payments as a result of losing their job. The Home Affordable Unemployment Program (UP) requires participating servicers to grant qualified unemployed borrowers a forbearance period during which their mortgage payments are temporarily reduced or suspended while they look for employment. At the end of this forbearance period, if the homeowner receives a HAMP modification, the forborne amount is capitalized onto the unpaid principal balance.

As of December 31, 2012, more than 30,000 UP forbearance plans had been started.

Homeowner Outreach

Treasury has continued its outreach initiatives to help homeowners who may be eligible for assistance through MHA and other programs.

"Help for Homeowners" Outreach Events

During 2012, Treasury, along with its partners at HUD conducted 18 "Help for Homeowners" outreach events across the country. These events provided struggling homeowners with the opportunity to speak directly with their mortgage servicer and trained housing counselors to learn more about the options that are available to them. Many of these events also include roundtable discussions with local leaders on broader issues facing the housing market.

As of December 31, 2012, there had been a total of 80 "Help for Homeowners" outreach events in more than 50 cities. These events have been attended by more than 70,000 homeowners.

Homeowner Outreach Events by Metropolitan Area as of December 31, 2012

1 Outreach Event
2 Outreach Events
3 - 6 Outreach Events

Top 10 Metropolitan Areas by Number of Events			
Metropolitan Area	Number of Events	Metropolitan Area	Number of Events
1 South Florida	6	6 Boston	3
2 Phoenix	5	7 Detroit	3
3 Washington, DC	5	8 Las Vegas	3
4 Atlanta	4	9 New York City	3
5 San Francisco Bay Area	4	10 Sacramento	3

Foreclosure Prevention Assistance Campaign

On December 12, 2012, Treasury, HUD, and the Ad Council unveiled the third and final phase of the Foreclosure Prevention Assistance Public Service Advertising (PSA) campaign. The campaign is intended to increase awareness of the MHA program's free resources and assistance for struggling homeowners. The PSAs, which are available in English and Spanish, direct homeowners to visit MakingHomeAffordable.gov or call 888-995-HOPE (4673) for free access to HUD-approved housing experts who are available to speak one-on-one about solutions based on each family's individual circumstances — 24 hours a day, 7 days a week.[28]

---

[28] For additional information and to view videos from the PSA campaign, please visit:
http://www.makinghomeaffordable.gov/about-mha/psa-campaigns/Pages/default.aspx

MHA Enhancements

In early 2012, the Obama Administration announced several enhancements to MHA, which included the following:

Extending the MHA Deadline

To help more eligible homeowners enter the program, Treasury extended the application deadline for borrowers to participate in MHA until December 31, 2013. This is a one-year extension from the previous deadline. It also conforms to the extended deadline for the Home Affordable Refinance Program (HARP), which is a program established by the FHFA to help underwater borrowers refinance their mortgages.

Expanding Eligibility

The program's eligibility criteria were also expanded to help reach people who are struggling with additional debt such as second liens and medical bills. To achieve this, MHA now offers another evaluation opportunity with more flexible debt-to-income criteria.

Eligibility has also been extended to include properties that are currently occupied by a tenant or which the borrower intends to rent since rental properties are an important source of affordable housing for many communities.

Increasing Incentives for Principal Reduction

In early 2012, Treasury included a number of provisions to further encourage investors to consider reducing principal on mortgage modifications. These include:

- Tripling the incentives to investors for principal reduction on first liens – incentives under the new structure range from 18 to 63 cents on the dollar, depending on the delinquency status of the loan and the loan-to-value ratio;

- Doubling incentives for principal extinguishment on second liens – incentives under the new structure range from 12 to 42 cents on the dollar; and

- Offering principal reduction incentives for loans insured or owned by the GSEs.[29]

Seventy-one percent of all eligible non-GSE loans entering HAMP in December 2012 included a principal reduction feature. Additional information and details about the MHA expansion and extension can be found in a statement by Assistant Secretary Timothy Massad,[30] originally published on January 27, 2012.

---

[29] The FHFA has since declined to offer these principal reduction incentives.

[30] http://www.treasury.gov/connect/blog/Pages/Expanding-our-efforts-to-help-more-homeowners-and-strengthen-hard-hit-communities.aspx

Hardest Hit Fund®

The second major housing initiative under TARP is the Hardest Hit Fund (HHF) ®. This program allows participating states' housing finance agencies (HFAs) in the nation's hardest hit housing and unemployment markets to design innovative, locally-targeted foreclosure prevention programs. Treasury provides funds to participating HFAs so states can design and implement programs that meet their needs.

HHF Program Update

When the program began, states needed time to build their operations and refine their processes. Through HHF, participating states have created from scratch their own servicing centers to directly handle homeowner applications, evaluate homeowners for assistance, and provide support to homeowners transitioning from one type of assistance to another. Since then, Treasury has worked closely with all key stakeholders including state HFAs, mortgage servicers, the GSEs, and the FHFA to encourage them to work together to reach more homeowners through HHF programs.

Treasury has also held yearly HHF summits, most recently in September 2012, to facilitate the sharing of best practices and lessons learned among participating HFAs. There was substantial growth in the HHF in 2012, both in the numbers served and the dollars spent. With recent program and operational changes made by HFAs working closely with Treasury, OFS expects the pace of assistance to continue to accelerate throughout 2013.

As of December 31, 2012, all 18 states and the District of Columbia were operating HHF programs statewide and collectively had drawn $1.76 billion (approximately 23 percent) of the $7.6 billion allocated under the program. Each state draws down funds as they are needed. States have until December 31, 2017 to expend funds and must have exhausted at least 95 percent of their allocation before they can draw down additional funds.

Hardest Hit Fund Disbursements (2011 & 2012)

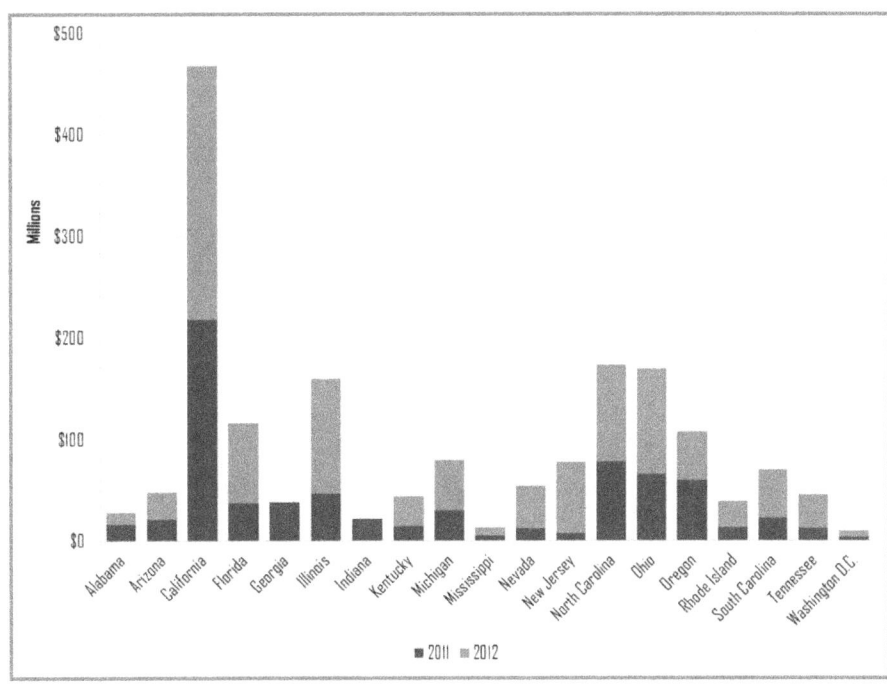

The most recent available performance reports indicate that participating HFAs have now assisted more than 77,000 homeowners.[31] They continue to innovate, develop new programs, and adapt existing programs to help homeowners amid changing market and economic conditions.

During 2012, Treasury approved several program changes submitted by state HFAs. Some examples include:

- Programs launched in both Arizona and Nevada that provide unmatched principal reduction in conjunction with a mortgage refinance, such as those provided through HARP;

- Programs in Arizona and California that provide unmatched principal reduction in conjunction with a loan recast or modification; and

- Programs in several states that are enabling modifications or recast loans in order to help homeowners achieve a lower payment. These programs are now available in Illinois, Ohio, Michigan, and South Carolina.

FHA Short Refinance Program

Treasury also continues to support the Federal Housing Administration (FHA) Short Refinance Program. Under this program, eligible borrowers who are current on their mortgage or complete a trial payment plan but owe more than their home is worth, can refinance into an FHA-insured loan if the lender writes off at least 10 percent of the existing loan.

Approximately $8.1 billion of TARP funds are committed to cover a share of losses on the refinanced loans. Additional TARP funds are available to provide incentive payments to extinguish second lien mortgages in order to facilitate refinancing of the first liens. As of December 31, 2012, there has not been substantial activity under the FHA Short Refinance Program and no disbursements for loss claim payments under the program have been made.

---

[31] The most recent available performance reports are through September 30, 2012.

The following is a brief discussion of why TARP was necessary and what it accomplished alongside the Federal Reserve and the FDIC's additional emergency measures. Additional information can be found in the TARP Two-Year Retrospective Report[32] and the 2012 Annual Report of the Financial Stability Oversight Council (FSOC).[33]

Why TARP was Necessary

TARP was launched when the American economy faced challenges on a scale not seen since the Great Depression. The crisis began in the summer of 2007 and gradually increased in intensity and momentum during 2008. The forces that brought about the crisis had built up over a long period of time. They included an unsustainable housing boom fueled in part by the easy availability of mortgages, excessive debt held by households and businesses, rapid growth of the nation's financial system, an outdated regulatory framework, and insensitivity to risk on the part of many investors.

On September 15, 2008, the crisis entered a new phase when Lehman Brothers filed for bankruptcy. That day, the stock market dropped by more than 500 points and there were signs of a generalized run on America's financial system. Markets that are essential for helping businesses and families meet their everyday financing needs were freezing up, threatening the availability of student loans, small business loans, auto loans and other forms of consumer lending. In short, the mechanisms that keep money flowing throughout our economy were failing.

By the end of September 2008, every major financial institution was threatened and many of them tried to shore up their balance sheets by shedding risky assets and hoarding cash. People were rapidly losing trust and confidence in the stability of America's financial system and the capacity of the government to contain the damage. Without immediate and forceful action by the Federal Government, the U.S. economy faced the risk of falling into a second Great Depression.

The government took a series of actions that included providing broad-based guarantees of bank accounts, money market funds, and liquidity through the Federal Reserve. However it was soon clear that the government needed additional tools to address a crisis on this scale. So in late September 2008, the Bush Administration proposed the law creating TARP. That measure was passed by Congress and signed into law by President Bush on October 3, 2008.

What TARP Helped Accomplish

Collectively, TARP and the government's other emergency measures were effective in preventing the collapse of our financial system, in restarting economic growth, and in restoring access to capital and credit. These programs were well designed and carefully managed. Because of this, we were able to limit the broader economic and financial damage.

The most important measure of the effectiveness of TARP and the government's other emergency programs is the impact they have had on restoring the nation's financial stability and restarting our economy. At the end of 2008, the American economy was contracting at an annual rate of more than nine percent and the pace of job losses was accelerating. In the first few months of 2009, more than

---

[32] http://www.treasury.gov/initiatives/financial-stability/reports/Documents/TARP%20Two%20Year%20Retrospective_10%2005%2010_transmittal%20letter.pdf

[33] http://www.treasury.gov/initiatives/fsoc/Documents/2012%20Annual%20Report.pdf

750,000 jobs were being lost per month. By the middle of 2009, after the government's emergency response programs had time to take effect, the rate of job losses began to slow and GDP began to recover. By early 2010, the economy began to add jobs. Although more work needs to be done to further strengthen growth, the emergency response programs put in place have helped the U.S. economy recover faster than many other nations dealing with similar crises in recent years.

International Economic Growth since 2008
Cumulative Growth in Real GDP since 2008 Q1

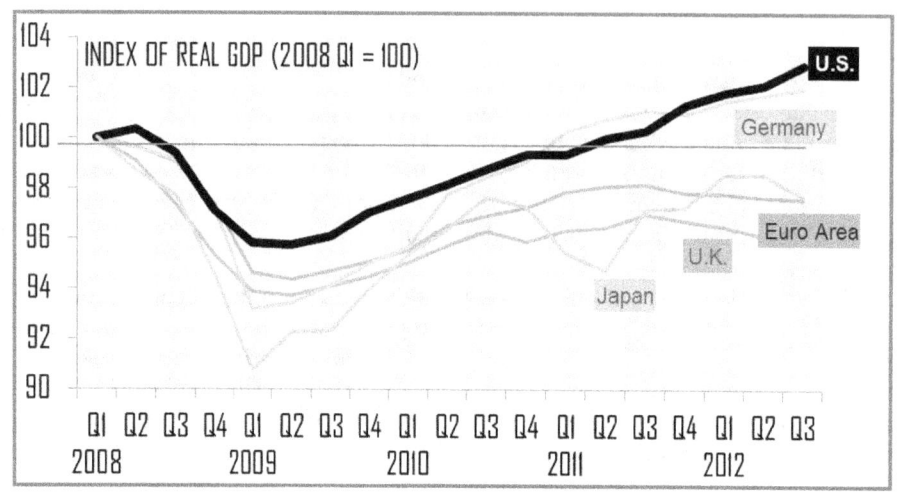

Private Sector Payroll Employment
Monthly Change, Seasonally Adjusted

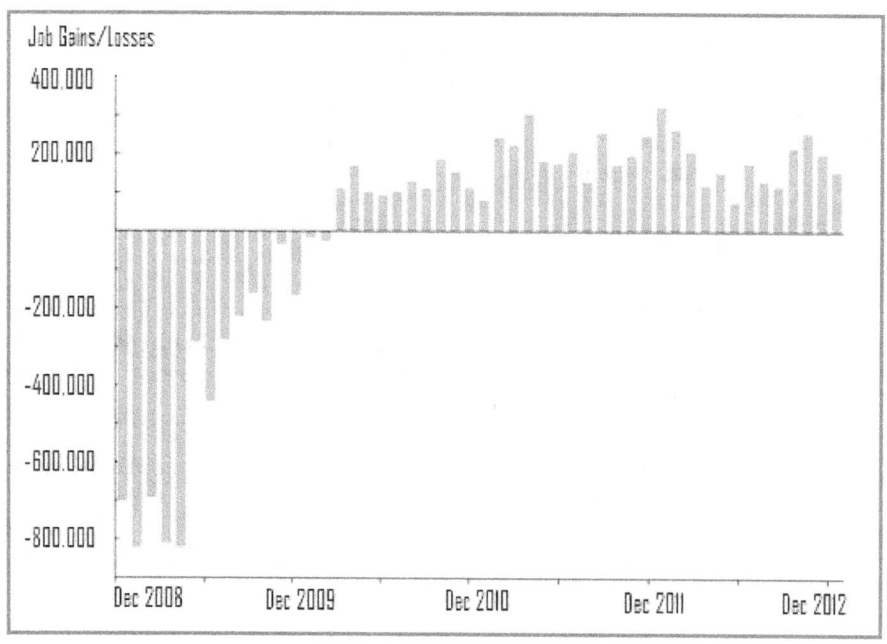

Timeline of the Financial Crisis and Response
S&P 500 Index, Five Year Bank CDS Spreads, and Net Tightening of Bank Lending Standards Since 2007

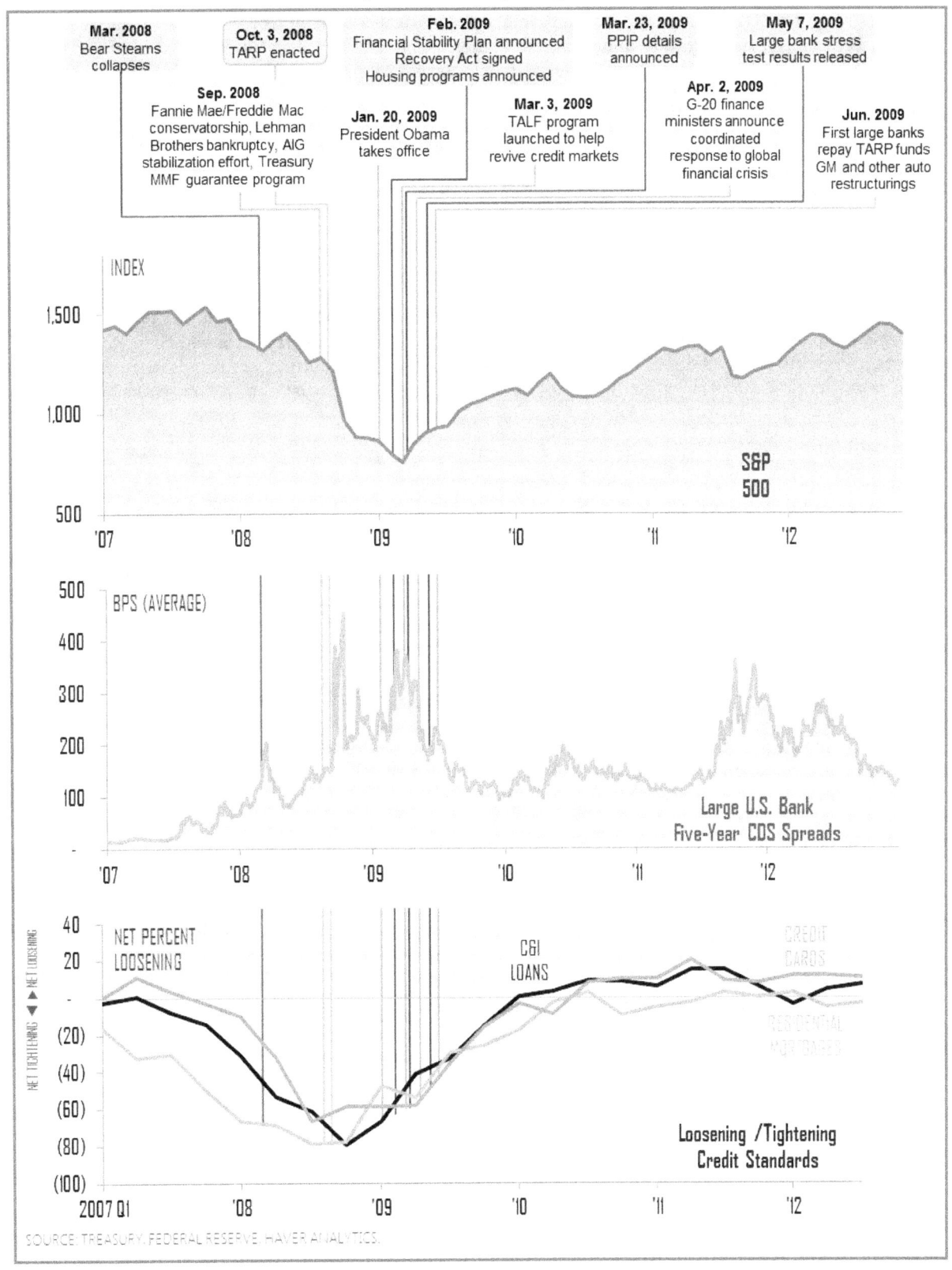

Mar. 2008
Bear Stearns collapses

Oct. 3, 2008
TARP enacted

Feb. 2009
Financial Stability Plan announced
Recovery Act signed
Housing programs announced

Mar. 23, 2009
PPIP details announced

May 7, 2009
Large bank stress test results released

Sep. 2008
Fannie Mae/Freddie Mac conservatorship, Lehman Brothers bankruptcy, AIG stabilization effort, Treasury MMF guarantee program

Jan. 20, 2009
President Obama takes office

Mar. 3, 2009
TALF program launched to help revive credit markets

Apr. 2, 2009
G-20 finance ministers announce coordinated response to global financial crisis

Jun. 2009
First large banks repay TARP funds GM and other auto restructurings

INDEX

1,500

1,000

500

S&P 500

'07   '08   '09   '10   '11   '12

500   BPS (AVERAGE)
400
300
200
100
-

Large U.S. Bank Five-Year CDS Spreads

'07   '08   '09   '10   '11   '12

40   NET PERCENT LOOSENING
20
-
(20)
(40)
(60)
(80)
(100)

C&I LOANS

CREDIT CARDS

RESIDENTIAL MORTGAGES

Loosening /Tightening Credit Standards

NET TIGHTENING ▼ ▲ NET LOOSENING

2007 Q1   '08   '09   '10   '11   '12

The crisis response also paved the way for Americans' retirement savings to recover. As measured by the performance of the S&P 500 index and retirement fund assets, these funds have continued to exhibit a measurable recovery from the lows they experienced in late 2008 and early 2009.

TARP helped enable the nation's banking system and credit markets to begin functioning again. When the Obama Administration took office, credit markets were all but frozen, making it extremely difficult for consumers and businesses to get loans. Availability of credit is critical for small businesses to grow and for consumers to make home improvements, buy a new car, or send their children to college. Soon after many TARP programs began to be implemented, borrowing costs declined for many businesses, homeowners, and municipalities. This helped to keep credit flowing throughout the economy.

Today our banking system is much stronger. Banks have higher capital levels, lower leverage, and the riskiest parts of the financial system no longer exist. Banks have strengthened their balance sheets by relying more on deposits and less on short-term wholesale funding. In addition, we have seen fewer bank failures since 2010 and the FDIC has shrunk their list of problem banks.

Reforming the System

During the financial crisis, the government's immediate priority was to stabilize a system in free-fall, limit the damage, and quickly restart economic growth. With the financial crisis having already taken a devastating toll in the form of lost jobs and lost savings, the government needed to take forceful actions that may have been unpopular but were necessary to stop the immediate crisis. Then President Obama worked with Congress to put reforms in place that would help address the underlying causes that led to the crisis in the first place.

In July 2010, Congress passed and President Obama signed the Dodd-Frank Wall Street Reform and Consumer Protection Act (Dodd-Frank) to strengthen safeguards for consumers and investors and to provide better tools for limiting risk in major financial institutions and throughout markets. Dodd-Frank provides a new framework for reining in excessive risk-taking on Wall Street and refocusing the financial system on activities that strengthen rather than threaten the health of the nation's economy. It includes:

- Providing stronger oversight of large, interconnected financial firms.
- Bringing together federal and state financial regulators to identify and respond to emerging threats to financial stability.
- Putting in place heightened prudential standards, including capital, liquidity and risk management standards to help ensure that these companies do not escape strong oversight or threaten financial stability.
- Giving the government new tools to wind down firms whose imminent failure could threaten the system.
- Bringing the derivatives market out of the shadows.
- Creating a dedicated watchdog for consumers in the form of the Consumer Financial Protection Bureau, so consumers have the information they need to make the financial decisions that are best for them.

Additional reforms are also moving forward. During 2012, the Federal Reserve, the OCC, and the FDIC jointly issued the finalized market risk capital rules. They also proposed new rules to bring domestic capital requirements more in line with international banking capital requirements (including aspects of Basel II, Basel 2.5, and Basel III). The implementation of these international agreements through domestic regulation is a key step in regulatory reform and for creating a safer and more resilient financial system going forward.

Executive Compensation

EESA, as amended by the American Recovery and Reinvestment Act (ARRA), set standards for executive compensation and corporate governance for all recipients of financial assistance under TARP.

Under ARRA, Treasury promulgated the Interim Final Rule on TARP Standards for Compensation and Corporate Governance (the Rule) on June 15, 2009. The Rule created the Office of the Special Master (OSM), which was delegated the responsibility to review and approve the compensation of top executives at firms that received exceptional assistance. In 2009, these firms were AIG, Bank of America, Citigroup, GM, Chrysler, Ally Financial and Chrysler Financial. As of December 31, 2012, only two exceptional assistance recipients – Ally Financial and GM – remain subject to the authority of the Special Master. The other five recipients of exceptional assistance have exited TARP.

The OSM conducted extensive reviews of executive compensation for 2009, 2010, 2011, and 2012 at the companies that continued to have exceptional assistance outstanding in each year, and imposed requirements based on the following key principles:

- For the top 25 individual pay packages: (i) limit cash salary, (ii) pay incentives in long-term restricted stock, (iii) limit perquisites and "other" compensation, and (iv) limit executive pension and retirement programs; and

- For the next 26-100 employees' compensation structures: (i) restrict short-term cash compensation, (ii) tie incentive compensation to real achievement, (iii) make sure compensation structures have a long-term focus, and (iv) align pay practices with shareholder and taxpayer interests.

The OSM has been effective at limiting compensation at the seven companies over which it had authority, while ensuring the companies were well-positioned to pay back the taxpayers' investments. The OSM cut the average cash pay for the top 25 executives at the seven companies that originally received exceptional assistance by more than 90 percent. The average total pay for the top 25 executives was cut by more than 50 percent. In addition, the OSM required that the majority of top 25 executive compensation be in the form of stock-based pay, the ultimate value of which will depend on the company's performance over the subsequent three-year period. The OSM also strictly limited prerequisites for these executives.

Actions in 2012

On April 6, 2012, the Acting Special Master for TARP Executive Compensation, Patricia Geoghegan, released the 2012 compensation determinations for the top 25 executives at the remaining companies that received exceptional assistance.[34] The overall CEO compensation packages payable by these firms were frozen compared to 2011 levels, although there has been some modification in the mix of stock salary and long-term restricted stock for the CEO group.

---

[34] The 2012 determinations can be found at: http://www.treasury.gov/press-center/press-releases/Pages/tg1525.aspx.

Transparency in TARP Programs

Treasury is committed to making sure that every TARP program is operating at the highest standards of transparency and accountability. This includes providing regular and comprehensive information about how TARP funds are being spent, who has received them and on what terms, and how much has been recovered to date.

OFS publishes a number of reports and other information on the status of TARP programs. These include the following reports:

- Monthly Report to Congress. Formerly known as the 105(a) report, this provides a monthly overview of how TARP funds have been used, how much has been recovered, the latest cost estimates for TARP, the program's operating expenses, and other information on the program.[35]

- Daily TARP Update. This report is a daily snapshot of the amount of funds disbursed and recovered to date for each individual TARP program, as well as additional financial information. This report is updated after each business day.[36]

- Annual Agency Financial Reports (AFRs). These annual reports contain the financial statements for TARP, the Government Accountability Office's (GAO) audit opinion on those financial statements, a separate opinion on OFS's internal controls over financial reporting, and results of GAO's tests of OFS's compliance with selected laws and regulations. The AFR is produced annually for the prior fiscal year and released during the last quarter of the calendar year.[37]

- Annual Citizens Reports on TARP. These reports contain information on the major activities conducted by OFS in implementing TARP. Citizens Reports are based on the Agency Financial Report. They cover the activities and results from the prior fiscal year and are released in the first quarter of the year.[38]

Treasury has also produced two retrospective reports on TARP previous to this one, on the second and third anniversaries of the program. These reports provide comprehensive information on the milestones achieved during the previous year in each TARP program, as well as TARP as a whole.[39]

In addition, Treasury prepares separate financial statements for TARP, which are audited annually by the GAO. In its first four years of operation, TARP's financial statements received unqualified audit opinions from its auditors at the GAO. OFS also received a Certificate of Excellence in Accountability Reporting (CEAR) from the Association of Government Accountants for fiscal years 2011, 2010 and the period ending September 30, 2009. These financial statements along with extensive information about the programs can be reviewed in OFS's AFR, referenced above.

These and many other reports on different aspects of TARP are available on the Financial Stability section of the Treasury.gov website.[40]

---

[35] http://www.treasury.gov/initiatives/financial-stability/reports/Pages/Monthly-Report-to-Congress.aspx

[36] http://www.treasury.gov/initiatives/financial-stability/reports/Pages/daily-tarp-reports.aspx

[37] http://www.treasury.gov/initiatives/financial-stability/reports/Pages/Annual-Agency-Financial-Reports.aspx

[38] http://www.treasury.gov/initiatives/financial-stability/reports/Pages/Citizens-Report-on-TARP.aspx

[39] http://www.treasury.gov/initiatives/financial-stability/reports/Pages/TARP-Annual-Retrospectives.aspx

Treasury is equally committed to ensuring that TARP's housing initiatives are being implemented to the highest level of transparency. OFS regularly publishes the following major reports that provide the latest financial and performance information about Treasury's housing programs:

- MHA Program Performance Report.[41] This is a monthly report containing detailed metrics on the MHA program. Once per quarter, this report is expanded to include detailed assessments of the performance of servicers participating in MHA.

- Monthly Housing Scorecard.[42] This is a monthly report that is produced jointly by Treasury and the U.S. Department of Housing and Urban Development detailing the health of the nation's housing market. It is generally released during the first week of each month.

- HAMP Activity by Metropolitan Statistical Area.[43] Published monthly in conjunction with the MHA Program Performance Report, this includes a detailed breakdown of mortgage modification activity in different metropolitan areas of the nation.

- Making Home Affordable Data Files.[44] These data files include loan-level data on the characteristics of program participants before and after entering HAMP. Treasury takes steps to safeguard the anonymity of individual borrowers when compiling these files.

- HAMP Application Activity by Servicer.[45] As required by the Dodd-Frank Wall Street Reform and Consumer Protection Act, this report shows the number of requests received, processed, approved, and denied by each participating servicer. It is published monthly.

- HHF State-by-State Information.[46] Treasury makes available the latest state-by-state information from HFAs that are administering local programs under the Hardest Hit Fund. Visitors to Treasury's website can also find each state's plan, contract agreements, and their latest quarterly report.

---

[40] http://www.treasury.gov/initiatives/financial-stability/reports/Pages/default.aspx

[41] http://www.treasury.gov/initiatives/financial-stability/reports/Pages/Making-Home-Affordable-Program-Performance-Report.aspx

[42] http://www.treasury.gov/initiatives/financial-stability/reports/Pages/Monthly-Housing-Scorecard.aspx

[43] http://www.treasury.gov/initiatives/financial-stability/reports/Pages/HAMP-Report.aspx

[44] http://www.treasury.gov/initiatives/financial-stability/reports/Pages/mha_publicfile.aspx

[45] http://www.treasury.gov/initiatives/financial-stability/reports/Pages/HAMP-Servicer.aspx

[46] http://www.treasury.gov/initiatives/financial-stability/TARP-Programs/housing/Pages/Program-Documents.aspx

EESA initially authorized up to $700 billion for TARP. At that time, many believed that taxpayers would lose that entire amount. In fact however, as of December 31, 2012, $418 billion was disbursed under TARP and the vast majority of that has already been recovered.

Estimated lifetime cost figures for TARP are updated quarterly in conjunction with the Office of Management and Budget (OMB). The latest available data is reported through December 31, 2012. As of that date, American taxpayers had already recovered $387.46 billion, representing nearly 93 percent of the TARP funds disbursed. TARP's bank investment programs alone have already earned more than $23 billion in positive returns for taxpayers.

According to Treasury and OMB's latest estimates, the expected overall cost of TARP will be $55.5 billion, using asset prices as of December 31, 2012.[47] And when Treasury's other interests in AIG are factored in, Treasury estimated that the combined net cost will be approximately $38 billion. The investment programs under TARP collectively, together with Treasury's overall AIG holdings are expected to break even or yield a small gain when they are fully wound down. Therefore, the total program cost of TARP is expected to be roughly equal to the amount that is ultimately disbursed to help homeowners avoid foreclosure—money that was never intended to be returned.

TARP was only one part of a broader federal response to the financial crisis. The latest estimates available indicate that the overall financial stability programs that Treasury, the Federal Reserve, and the FDIC put in place during the crisis are likely to result in an overall positive financial return for taxpayers in terms of direct fiscal cost.[48] When taken together with the Federal Government's other emergency response programs, taxpayers now stand to earn a significant positive return from the financial crisis response.

All recovered funds are deposited in the U.S. Treasury and go towards reducing the national debt.

---

[47] The ultimate lifetime cost of the TARP investments will be impacted by share prices of its common stock in GM, AIG, and the value of its CPP investments. Treasury will continue to manage its investments in order to balance speed of exit with maximizing returns for taxpayers.

[48] Additional information can be found in "The Financial Crisis Response in Charts," published by Treasury in April 2012 and available at: http://www.treasury.gov/resource-center/data-chart-center/Documents/20120413_FinancialCrisisResponse.pdf

Links for Further Information

Glossary of Terms[49]

The Office of Financial Stability's website[50]

U.S. Department of the Treasury's website[51]

U.S. Department of the Treasury's Press Center[52]

The Response to the Financial Crisis in Charts[53] – These charts provide a more comprehensive update on the impact of the combined actions of the Treasury, the Federal Reserve, and the FDIC.

---

[49] http://www.treasury.gov/initiatives/financial-stability/glossary/Pages/Default.aspx

[50] http://www.treasury.gov/initiatives/financial-stability/Pages/default.aspx

[51] http://www.treasury.gov/Pages/default.aspx

[52] http://www.treasury.gov/press-center/Pages/default.aspx

[53] http://www.treasury.gov/connect/blog/Pages/financial-crisis-response-in-charts.aspx

www.ingramcontent.com/pod-product-compliance
Lightning Source LLC
Chambersburg PA
CBHW081311180526
45170CB00007B/2658